EPITAPHS
IN THE
OLD BURYING-GROUND AT DEERFIELD, MASSACHUSETTS

C. ALICE BAKER AND EMMA L. COLEMAN

HERITAGE BOOKS
2007

HERITAGE BOOKS
AN IMPRINT OF HERITAGE BOOKS, INC.

Books, CDs, and more—Worldwide

For our listing of thousands of titles see our website
at
www.HeritageBooks.com

Published 2007 by
HERITAGE BOOKS, INC.
Publishing Division
65 East Main Street
Westminster, Maryland 21157-5026

Copyright © 1924 C. Alice Baker and Emma L. Coleman

All rights reserved. No part of this book may be reproduced or transmitted in any form or by any means, electronic or mechanical, including photocopying, recording or by any information storage and retrieval system without written permission from the author, except for the inclusion of brief quotations in a review.

International Standard Book Number: 978-0-7884-3507-2

GRAVESTONE OF LIEUT. MEHUMAN HINSDELL (1736)
THE FIRST MALE CHILD BORN IN DEERFIELD

GRAVESTONES OF JOHN STEBBINS (1760) AND HIS WIFE MARY (1733)

GRAVESTONE OF MRS. EUNICE WILLIAMS (1704)

THE BURYING-GROUND AT DEERFIELD, MASSACHUSETTS

INTRODUCTION

ACTING upon the request made several years ago by the New England Historic Genealogical Society of Boston, Miss C. Alice Baker of Cambridge and Deerfield began the work of copying the inscriptions on the gravestones of the old burying ground in this town. The town records of New England often lack facts which the graveyards can supply, and when a stone disappears—as indeed happened between the beginning and ending of this copying—the record is lost.

For this purpose the Genealogical Society is always glad to furnish suggestions as to methods, to supply durable paper and to care for manuscript copies in its library.

In this case, the manuscript has been held until the Pocumtuck Valley Memorial Association found a fitting time to print. Many hands have, from time to time, helped with the copying, but the undersigned, who after Miss Baker's death, assumed the obligation of finishing the work acknowledges especially the help of Miss Lucy Pratt.

EMMA L. COLEMAN

Frary House, November, 1923

DEERFIELD EPITAPHS

Allen ? 1696

M A DYED
NOVEM 7
ANNO 1696

The only "M. A." found in Mr. Sheldon's Genealogies in the "History of Deerfield," or in the "Vital Statistics," who might have died in 1696, is Mercy Allen, dau. of Samuel and Mercy (Wright.) She was born 24 June 1695.

Allen, 1719.

HERE LYES THE
BODY OF Mrs MARTHA
ALLEN DEC'^{d}, FEB^{ry}
Y^e 26th 1719/20
IN Y^e 23^d YEAR
OF HER AGE

Dau. Ebenezer Wells of Hatfield, m. to Edward Allen Feb. 4, 1719/20.

Near this headstone are two small sunken stones, marked E. A. and R. A. probably foot stones.

Allen, 1746

In memory of
Mr Samuel Allen who
Fell by the Indian Savage^s
Augus^t ye 25th 1746
Valliantly Defending his
Own Life & Childrens in
ye 45th Year of his Age.

Listen to me ye Mortal men Beware, That you engage no more in direfull War, By means of War my Soul from Earth is fled, My Body Log'd in Mansions of the Dead.

S. of Edward and Mercy (Painter)

Allen, 1754

Mr. Sam Allen
Died. July 24
1754, in the
24th Year of
his age.

S. of Joseph and Hannah (Cles son) of Northampton.

Allen, 1765

In Memory of
Miss Mer^{c}y Alle^n
Dau^r to Mr Sam-
uel & Mrs Hann-
ah Allen who
Died Octr 9th 1765
in ye 25 Year of
her Age

Allen, 1767

In Memory of Miss
Chloe Allen Dau^r
to Mr Samuel & M^{rs}
Hannah Allen wh^o
died Octr 25th 1767
in ye 34th Year of
her Age

Allen, 1771

In Memory of M^{rs}
Hannah Wife of
Mr Samuel Allen
who died March
8th 1771 in ye 69th
Year of her Age

*Dau. of Deacon Eliezer and Judith
(Smead) Hawks.*

Allen, 1773

Eliel Allen Son of
Mr Caleb & M^{rs}
Judath Allen who
died Augst ye 5th
1773 in ye 3^d
Year of his Age

*Caleb was s. of Samuel and Han-
nah (Hawks). Judith, dau. of
Eleizer and Margaret (Allen)
Hawks.*

Allen, 1775

Asaph Allen Son of
Mr Caleb & M^{rs}
Judath Allen who
died Septr 25th 1775
in ye 3^d Year of his
Age

Ames, 1798

Samuel Son of
Mr Ebenezer &
Mrs Elizabeth
Ames who
died Sept. 30th
1798, in the 4th
Year of his Age

Amsden, 1742

In Memory of
Mr. John Ams-
den who Died
July 3, 1742
in ye 55 Year
of his Age.

S. of John of Cambridge and Hatfield and Elizabeth. Was drowned at Cheapside.

Amsden, 1746

In Memory of
Oliver & Simeon
Amsden who Died
Augst 25 1746
Oliver aged 18
Simeon aged
9 Years

Sons of John and Mary (Cowles). Killed at Bars Fight.

Arms, 1729-1731

HERE
LYES BURIED
THE BODY OF
Mr WILLIAM
ARMS WHO
DEC^d AUGUST
Y^e 25 1731
IN Y^e 77th
YEAR OF
HIS AGE

Amsden, 1757

Mrs Mary Wife
of Mr John Ams
den Died Jan'^{y}
27 1757 In
ye 58 year of
her age

Dau. of Samuel Cowles of Hatfield and Sarah (Hubbard).

Amsden, 1794

This Monument
is Erected in
Memory of Mr John Amsden
who died Oct^r
10th 1794 in the 73
Year of his Age.

Ware I so tall to reach the Pole,
Or Grasp the Ocean with my Span,
I must be measur'd by my Soul,
The Mind is the Standard of the Man.

S. of John and Mary (Cowles).

HERE
LYES BURIED
THE BODY OF
Mrs JOANNA ARMS
WIFE TO M^r
WILL^m ARMS
WHO DEC^d
NOV^r Y^e 22^d 1729
IN Y^e 77th YEAR
OF HER AGE

Dau. of John and Elizabeth Hawks of Hadley.

Armes, 1736

HERE LYES Y^e BODY OF
Mrs ESTHER ARMES WIFE
TO Mr DANIEL ARMES
DEC^d DECEM^r Y^e 17th
1736 IN Y^e 41st YEAR
OF HER AGE

Dau. Ebenezer and Esther (Catlin) Smead.

Arms, 1751

Here lyes the
Body of Mrs.
Hannah Arms
Wife of Mr. John
Arms Who Died
Octr. 20th 1751.
In the 63^d Year
of her age.

Dau. of Thomas and Hannah (Coleman) Nash of Hatfield.

Arms, 1753

In Memory of
Mr. JOHN ARMS.
Who Died on
Septemb'^r 20th
1753, In ye 74th
Year of his age.

S. of William and Joanna (Hawks).

Arms, 1753

In Memory
of Mr. DANI-
EL ARMS, Who
Died Sep^t 28
1753. In y^e
67th Year of
his age

S. of William and Joanna (Hawks).

Arms, 1756

Noah; Son of Mr.
William Arms Jun
Died Sep'^t 25
AD 1756. aged
3 Years & 6
Months

S. of William and Elizabeth (Belding of Hatfield).

Arms, 1757

Phinehas Son of
Mr. William & Mrs.
Elizabeth Arms
Died Nov. 25 AD
1757 aged 1
Year & 7 Months
Their Child Sub
mit Died Nov. 27
1757 aged 10 days

Arms, 1768

On the 12th Day of May 1768, the Home of Mr. William Arms was Consumed by Fire And his Wife Mrs. Rebecca Arms unhappily perished in the Flames in the 70th year of her Age

She was one who Feared God & Lov'd the Redeemer, was a singular Example of Piety, who by a devout walk was a Bright Ornament to the Christian Religion, And her Death Great Gain

Dau. of Thomas and Hannah (Coleman) Nash of Hatfield.

Arms, 1773

In Memory of Mrs Rebekah Wife of Mr Jonathan Arms who Died Novr ye 16th 1773 in ye 31st Year of her Age

Death is A debt to Nature due Which I have paid & so must you.

Dau. of Samuel Hinsdale of Greenfield and Rebecca (Leonard) of Northampton.

Arms, 1771

In Memory of Mrs Experience the Wife of Lieu^{t} Elijah Arms, she Died Decr ye 28th 1771 in ye 32nd Year of her Age.

Here lyes the Children of Lieu^{t} Elijah & Mrs Experience Arms.

Lucinda Born Decr. ye 12th 1771 Died Febry ye 25th 1772. } A Dautr Born Sept. ye 15th 1765 & Died the same Day

Dau. of Nathaniel Hawks and Martha (Wait) of Hatfield.

Arms, 1774

In Memory of Mr. WILLIAM ARMS Who Died Sept 27 1774. In the 82 Year of his Age

Son of William 1

Arms, 1770, 1783

A double Stone

In Memory	In Memory
of Dorothy	of Lucinda
Arms daught^r	Arms daught^r
To Mr Jon^a &	to Mr Jon^a & M^{rs}
Mrs Eunice	Rebekah
Arms who	Arms who
died ag^t 28th	died July 7th
1770 aged 14	1783 in ye 11th
days	Year of her age

Mrs. Rebecca was b. Hinsdale
Mrs. Eunice was dau. of Aaron Lyman of Belchertown.

Arms, 1784

Here lies inter'd
the Body of M^r
Daniel Arms
who died May 7th 1784
in ye 65th Year of his Age

Whatever Farce ye boastful hero plays
Virtue alone has Majesty in Death

S. of Daniel and Esther (Smead).

Arms, 1785, 1788

In Memory of Fanny Daut'r
of m^r Phineas & m^{rs} Liddia
Arms she died July 17th 1785
Aged 3 Years & 11 months
& 8 days, Fanny second
died January 15th 1788
Aged 4 months.

Phineas was s. of William (3) and Lydia, dau. of Philip Root of Montague and Abigail (Smead) of Greenfield.

Arms, 1794

In MEMORY of
Miss MIRIAM ARMS,
Daughter of Deacon
JONATHAN and M^{rs}
REBEKAH ARMS
who died, April 4th
1794, in the 23^{d} Year
of her Age

<small>Virtue alone has Majes
ty   in   Death</small>

Arms, 1794

In Memory of M^r
William Arms
who died May 10th
1794, in the 70th
Year of his Age.

<small>An honest Man's the noblest
work of God.</small>

S. of William (2) and Rebecca (Nash).

Arms 1798

To Perpetuate the
Memory of M^{rs}
Mary Arms Con-
-sort of Mr Daniel
Arms, who died
March 20 1798,
in the 78th Year of
her Age.

<small>The thought of death is the
directing helm of Life,
and he bespeaks a wreck
Who lays it aside.</small>

Dau. of John and Mary Stebbins.

Arms, 1804

In Memory of
Mrs. Elizabeth Arms,
Consort of
Mr. William Arms,
who departed this
Life Feb. 24 1804, aged
81 Years.

<small>Your eyes are upon me,
And I am not.</small>

Dau. of Samuel Belding of Hatfield and Elizabeth (Dickinson) of Springfield.

Ashley, 1738

William the
Son of ye Rev'd
Mr Jonathan &
Mrs Dorothy
Ashley who dye^d
March ye 17 1738
Aged 9 Months.

Ashley, 1742

William ye Son
of ye Rev'd M^r
Jonathan & M^{rs}
Dorothy Ashley
who dyed Sep^t
the 28 1742
Aged 17 mo^{n}ths

Ashley, 1748

> In Memory of Solomo^n
> Son of the Rev^d M^r
> Jonathan Ashley &
> Mrs Dorothy his wife
> Born Sep^t ye 13th 1747
> Died June ye 23rd 1748

Ashley, 1772

> Here lies Intered
> William Son of
> Jonathan Ashley Esqr
> & Mrs Tirxah his wife,
> Born Sep^t ye 28th 1772
> Died Octo^{br} ye 7th 1772.

Ashley, 1779

> Nancy
> Daughter to
> Elihu & Mary
> Cook Ashley
> died Janr^y 6th 1779
> Aged 6 Months

This and the following are two of three baby graves, which lie side by side; all having coffins cut upon the surface of the stones.

Ashley, 1780

> Elisabeth Matild^a
> Daughter of Jon^a
> Ashley Esqr. &
> Tirzah his wife
> Died May 19th
> 1780 aged 3 weeks.

Ashley, 1780

> In Memory of Rev
> Jonathan Ashley,
> who died August 28,
> 1780, in the 68 Year of
> his Age, & 48 of his Min-
> -istry, leaving a Name dear
> to his Friends, & A'quaintan'e
> for his social kind & pleas-
> -ing Deportment, in particu-
> -lar for his Zeal in the Cause
> of Christianity, which united
> with Superior Knowledge & a
> ready Utterance of
> Moral & Divine Truths ren-
> -dered him a shining light
> in the Station, where God
> had placed him

S. of Jonathan and Abigail (Stebbins).

Ashley, 1787

> To PERPETUAT^e
> the MEMORY of
> JONATHAN
> ASHLEY Esqr
> who died May 30th
> 1787 in ye 49th Year
> of his Age.
>
> Friends so well
> embraced at Heart
> Nought but Death
> [The fourth line has been covered
> by resetting the stone].

A tory, s. of Rev. Jon^a. His wife, Tirzah, was dau. of David Field, an ardent patriot.

Ashley, 1808

In Memory of the
W^d Dorothy Ashley
Relict of the Rev
Jonathan Ashley,
An agreeable com-
-panion, an Affectio-
-nate Mother & the
Christians Friend,
who died Sept. 20,
1808 aged 95
Years

Dau. of Rev. William Williams of Hatfield and Christian (Stoddard).

Bardwell-Bordwell, 1771

In Memory of
Mr Samuel Bordwell
he Died March ye 18th 1771
in the 86th Year
of his Age.

Come hither Mortals, cast an eye
then go thy way, prepare to Die,
here read thy Doom
for Die thou must,
one Day like me be turn'd to dust.

S. of Robert of Hatfield and Mary (Gull).

Bardwell, 1775

In Memory of
Mrs Martha Wife
of Mr Samuel
Bardwell who
died Feb. 11th
1777 in the 82nd
Year of her Age.

Dau. Edward, of Suffield and Mercy (Painter) Allen.

Bardwell, 1781

In Memory of
Mr. Thomas Bardwell,
who departed this
Life on February
8th 1781˙ in the
Ninetyeth Year
of his Age.

S. of Robert and Mary (Gull).

Bardwell, 1783

In Memory of
Mrs. Sarah Bardwell˙
Relict of
Mr. Thomas Bardwell
who died January
ye 12th 1783; in
the 82^d Year
of her Age.

Dau. of John and Sarah (perhaps Wait) Belding of Hatfield.

Bernard (Barnard), 1695

    HERE LYES
    BURED Y^e BODY
    OF JOSEPH
    BERNARD AGED
    45 YEARS DEC^t
    SEPTEMBER Y^e
    6th 1695

S. of Francis and Frances (Foote | Dickinson). The oldest stone.

Bernard, 1720

    HERE LYES INTERRED
    Y^e BODY OF M^{rs}
    SAR^{a}H BERNARD WIFE
    TO Mr SAMUEL BERNAR^d
    DEC^d AUGUST Y^e 1st
    1720 IN Y^e 33
    YEAR OF HER AGE
    & SAMUEL SON TO SAID
    SAMUEL & SARAH BERNAR^d
    DECEASED Y^e 4th DAY
    OF AUGUST 1720
    AGED 13 DAYES

Bernard, 1736

    HERE LYES Y^e BODY OF
    EBENEZER BERNARD
    JUN^r Y^e SON OF M^r
    EBENEZER & M^{rs}
    ELIZABETH BERNARD
    AGED 17th YEARS
    WANTING 24 D^s DIED 31
    JANUARY 1736

Barnard, 1744

    ANNA FOSTER
    BARNARD, the
    Daughter of M^r
    EBENEZER & M^{rs}
    ELIZABETH BARNARD
    Died May 30th
    1744: Aged
    11 years.

Barnard, 1753

    HERE LIES THE BODY OF
    Mrs ELIZABETH BARNARD,
    THE WIFE OF
    Mr EBENEZER BARNARD;
    SHE DIED AUGUST 4th
    1753 IN Y^e 59th YEAR
    OF HER AGE·

Dau. of James and Anna (Lane) Foster of Roxbury.

Barnard, 1764

Memento Mori
In Memory of M^r
EBENEZER BARNARD who
Dec^d July ye 20th AD
1764 in ye 68th
Year of his Age.

S. of Joseph and Sarah (Strong) of Northampton.

Barnard, 1772

Mrs, Thankfull,
consort of Mr, Joseph
Barnard, died Nov. 3d,
1772. in the 53d, year of
her age

Dau. of Ebenezer and Thankful (Barnard) Sheldon. Joseph and Thankful (above) were cousins.

Barnard, 1772

Miss Rachel,
daughter of Mr. Joseph
and Mrs, Thank'l Barnard,
died Nov. 16th, 1772.
in the 17th, year of her
age.

Barnard, 1775

In Memory of
Elihu Son of M^r
Salah & Mr^s Elisabeth
Barnard he Dec^d
June ye 20th 1775

Salah was s. of Ebenezer and Elizabeth (Foster). Elizabeth was dau. of Jeremiah and Mary (Cooley) Nims.

Barnard, 1782

In Memory of
Elihu Son of M^r
Salah & M^{rs}
Elisabeth Barnard
he Dec^d Mar^h y^e
18th 1782 Aged
7 Months & 27 D

Barnard, 1785

Mr, Joseph Barnard,
died December 17th, 1785.
in the 68th, year of his age

S. of Ebenezer and Elizabeth (Foster) of Roxbury.

Barnard, 1790

Doctor Ebenezer Barnard,
died April 14th, 1790.
in the 45th, year of his age.

S. of Joseph and Thankful (Sheldon). Harvard College 1766.

Beamon, 1711/12

HERE LYES Y^e
BODY OF
SIMON BEAMO^n
AGED 54. YEAR^s
DEC^t Y^e 19th OF
FEBRUARY
1711/12

S. of Simon of Springfield and Alice (Young).

Beamon, 1739

HERE LYES Y^e BODY OF
Mrs HANNAH BEAMON
WHO DEPARTED
THIS LIFE Y^e 13th OF
MAY, 1739.
IN Y^e 94th YEAR
OF HER AGE.

Dau. of Francis Barnard; wife of Dr John Westcarr of Hadley and Simon Beaman. Deerfield's first school-dame.

Belding, 1730, 1731

DAN^l BEL^d
IN DYE^d
IVNE Y^e 1
AT 10 MOVNTH
OULD 1730 AND
DAN^l IN IEN Y^e
1 1731 AN INF-
ANT

Two infant sons of Daniel and Esther (Smith) Belding; the first Daniel dying in June, the second in January. The stone is rough, irregular in shape and rudely cut, not the work of a stone-man.

Billings, 1785

Here is reposited
the Remains of
Mrs Rebekah Consort
of Doct^r Edward
Billings who died
of the small Pox
Septr 13th AD 1785
aetat 24

He mourns the dead
Who lives as they desire

Dau. of Jonathan and Rebecca (Hinsdale) Arms.

Birge, 1778

In Memory of
John son of M^r
John & Mrs Esth
er Birge who di
ed July 24th 1778
Aged 1 year & 8 M
onths & 10 Days.

Birge, 1785

In Memory of
Bohan son of Mr.
John & Mrs Esth-
er Birge who dep
arted this Life
Septr 20th 1785 aged
13 years & five
Days

Birge, 1803

Esther Birge
died
Nov. 13. 1803,
in the 66 year of
her age
By Son J. B.

A John and John Jr. were of Northampton. She was received from the Church of Spencer.

Bradley, 1792

Philo Son of
Mr Joseph &
Mrs Lydia
Bradley who
died Jan. 2nd
1792 in the 6th
Month of his
Age.

Lydia was dau. of Benj. Munn and m. 1st. John Saxton.

Bull, 1759

In Memory of
Elisabeth Dau^r
of Mr John &
Mrs Mary
Bull, Born
August ye 5th
died Septr y^e
14th 1759.

John was s. of Nehemiah and Elizabeth (Partridge). Mary was dau. of John and Mary (Munn) Catlin.

Bull, 1795

Here lies
the Remains of
Mr. Justin Bull,
who died
June 5, 1795,
Aged 61 years.

Tender were his Feelings;
The Christian was his Friend
Honest were his Dealings
And happy was his End.

S. of Nehemiah and Elizabeth (Partridge) of Hatfield.

Burt, 1732, 1752

In Memory of
Lieu^t Jonathan Burt,
he Died Sep^t ye 17th 1752.
in the 46th Year of
his Age

At the right hand
lies A Dau^{tr} Born
March ye 6th 1732
& Died the same Day

S. of Henry and Elizabeth (Warriner).

Burt, 1752

In Memory of
Mr Jonathan Burt
Son of Lieu^t Jonathan
& Mrs Bridget Burt,
he died Sepr ye 21st 1752
in the 23rd Year
of his Age

Burt, 1752

MRS. RACHEL
Daught^r of
Lieut. Jonathan
& Mrs. Bridget
Burt: who Died
Octob^r 20th
1752 Aged 17
years & 8 Mo

Burt, 1792

In Memory of
Mrs Bridget the
Wife of Lieut
Jonathan Burt
Deseas'd who died
April ye 12 1792,
in the 84th Year
of her Age.

Dau. of Dr. John and Bridget (Cook) Barnard of Hadley.

Burt, 1793

Alva Son of
Lieut Ithemer
& Mrs Prudenc^e
Burt who died
March 23^d 1793
Aged 15 Days

Ithemar was s. of Daniel. Prudence, dau. of Thomas Dickinson.

Burt, 1797

In Memory of Miss
Bridget the Dau^r, of
Lieut Jonathan and
Mrs Bridget Burt
She died Decr 20
1797, in the 52nd
Year of her Age

Catling, 1758

In Memory of
Capt John Catling who Died
Sep^t 24, 1758,
Aged 56 Years

S. of Joseph and Hannah (Sheldon).

Catlin, 1760

In Memory of M^{rs}
Thankfull the wife
to Mr Nathan Catlin
she Died Augst ye 23^d
1760 in ye 31st Year
of her Age

*Dau. of Timothy and Thankful
(Ackley) Foster of Wallingford,
Conn.*

Catlin, 1763

In Memory of
Mrs Mary Catlin
the virtuous Relict of
Capt John Catlin
She died Novr 10th AD 1763
Aged 58 years.

*Dau. of Benjamin and Thankful
(Nims) Munn.*

Catlin, 1766, 1772

In Memory of M^r
John Catlin he Died
Decr ye 1st 1766. in the
80th Year of his Age.

In Memory of M^{rs}
Jemima the Widow of
Mr John Catlin she
Died Feb^{ry} ye 6th 1772. in
the 76th Year of her Age.

Depart my friends, dry up your tears
here we must lie, till Christ appears.

*S. of John and Mary (Baldwin).
Dau. of Edward and Mercy
(Painter) Allen.*

Catlin, 1777

In Memory of
Henry. Son of
Mr Seth & M^{rs}
Abigail Catlin he
Dec^d Augst ye 9th
1777 Aged 2 years
& 6 Months.

Catlin, 1793

In Memory of
Mr Nathan Catlin
who died Decr 7th
1793 in the 77th
Year of his
Age.

S. of John and Jemima (Allen).

Catlin, 1798

IN
MEMORY
of
Seth Catlin Esq^e
who died
March 19th 1798,
aged
Sixty three years.

S. of John and Mary (Munn).

Catlin, 1805

M^rs
Abigail, Relic
of Seth Catlin
Esq. died Dec. 6
1805: Æt. 67

Dau. of Aaron Denio, the name given in Deerfield to Rene de Noyon. She was named for her grandmother, Abigail Stebbins.

Champney, 1903

James Wells Champney
Born
July 16. 1843.
Died
May 1. 1903.

S. of James and Sarah (Wells).

Chandler, 1775

Amariah Son
of Mr Moses &
Mrs Perses
Chandler wh°
died Octr 27th
1775 in ye 2^d
Year of his
Age.

Amariah's mother was born Harris.

Childs, 1727

Here Lyes ye Body
of Mrs Hannah
Childs Wife to
Mr Samuel Childs
Who Dec^d May
16. 1727 in ye 39th
Year of Her Age

Dau. of Joseph and Sarah (Strong) Barnard.

Childs, 1752

Mrs. Sarah
Wife of Dea^c
SAM'^l CHILDS
Died March
21. 1752. In
ye 64 year
of her age.

Dau. of Philip and Sarah (Hawks) Mattoon and widow of Zechariah Field of Northfield.

Childs, 1753.

In Memory of
RACHEL Dau'^tr
of Mr. Asa & Mrs
Rhoda Childs,
Who, Died June
8th, 1753, aged
5 Years & 3 M.

Asa was s. of Samuel and Hannah (Barnard). Mrs. Rhoda was dau. of Capt. Benjamin and Thankful (Taylor) Wright of Northampton.

Childs, 1755

Simeon Son
of Mr. Samuel
& Mrs. Sarah
Childs Died
Dec. 12. 1755
Aged 2 Years
& 8 Months.

S. of Samuel and Sarah (Wright).

Childs, 1756

In Memory of
Deacon Samuel
Childs Who Di
ed March, 18th
1756. Aged
77 Years.

S. of Richard and Elizabeth (Crocker) of Barnstable.

Childs, 1756

In Memory of
Mr. Asa Childs
Who Died
June 28, AD.
1756. Aged
41 Years, 6 M.

S. of Samuel and Hannah (Barnard).

Childs, 1758

Experience Daut^r
of Mr; Samuel
Childs Died Sep^t
28. 1758. aged 1.
Year & 7 Months

Dau. of Samuel and Sarah (Wright).

Childs, 1760

In Memory of
Mr, David Childs
Who Died
May 8, 1760
in ye 43 Year
of his Age.

S. of Samuel and Hannah (Barnard).

Childs, 1760

David son of Mr.
David & Mrs.
Rebekah Childs,
Died June 13, 1760
in ye 11th year of
his Age

David Sr. was s. of Samuel. Rebecca was dau. of William Arms.

Childs, 1768, 1771

In Memory of the
Children of Mr Amzi
& Mrs Submit Chil-
ds, Elizabeth Died
April ye 29th 1768,
Aged 4 Months lies
at ye left hand. David
Wright Died May y^e
21st 1771. Aged 9 Days
lies at ye right hand.
*Amzi was s. of Samuel and Sarah
(Wright). Submit, dau. of
David and Elizabeth (Hitchcock)
Wright.*

Childs, 1770

In Memory of M^{rs}
Elisabath, the wife of
Mr Asa Childs, & Dau^{tr}
of Col^o.&Mrs Elisabath
Hawks, she Died Decem^r
ye 24th 1770, in y^e
32^d year of her
Age.

Childs, 1771

In Memory of Asa
Son of Mr Asa
& Mrs Elisabeth
Childs. he Died
Feb^{ry} ye 4th 1771
Aged 1 Year &
4 Months

Childs, 1771

In Memory of
Elisabeth Dau^{tr} of M^r
Asa & Mrs Elisabeth
Childs she Died
March ye 31st 1771
Aged 3 Months
& 15 Days

Childs, 1777

The remains
of two Child-
ren, of Mr
Samuel & Mrs
Mary Childs,
Israel died Aug'st
8, 1777, aged 4
Years. Experience
died August 2,
1777, Aged 2
Years.
*The mother, Mary, was dau. of
Jeremiah and Mary (Cooley)
Nims.*

Childs, 1782

In Memory of
Mr. Lemuel Childs
who Died April
23^d Anno Dom
1782 Aged 30
Years & 19 Days
S. of David and Rebecca (Arms).

Childs, 1786

In Memory of
Deacon
Samuel Childs,
who departed this
Life January 15th
1786. in the 74th
Year of his Age.

Death gives us more than was in Edon
lost,
This King of terrour is the Prince of Peace.

S. of Samuel and Hannah (Barnard).

Childs, 1797

In Memory of the
W^d Sarah Childs,
Relict of Deacon
Samuel Childs, who
died Nov. 26, 1797,
aged 84 Years.

Dau. of Judah and Mary (Hoyt) Wright.

Childs, 1799

To Perpetuate the
Memory of Miss
Esther Childs
Daughter of M^r
Samuel & M^{rs}
Eunice Childs
who died Jan 13
1799 Aged 25
Years

Mrs. Eunice was dau. of Noah and Esther (Scott) Wright.

Corse,

In memory of
JAMES CORSE
first of the name in America,
m. in Deerfield ab^t 1690,
d. May 15, 1696, aged ab^t 30
ELIZABETH, his wife,
| dau. of Mr John & Mary
(Baldwin) Catlin |
Captured Feb. 29, 1703/4,
| k. on the march to Canada,
aged ab^t 34 |

Children.
EBENEZER, b. Apr. 7, 1692
JAMES, b. Mar. 20, 1694
ELIZABETH, b. Feb. 4, 1696
was carried captive to Canada
and never came back.
| She m. at St. Lambert,
Nov. 6, 1712, |
Jean Dumontel.
| She m. (2) at St. Lambert,
Jan. 6, 1730 |
Pierre Monet.
She was the mother of 15 children
the last (twins) b. Apr. 12, 1737

This fine slate stone was placed by Mr. Charles Corss, of Lock Haven, Pennsylvania.

Dickinson, 1740

In memory of
Mrs. HANNAH
Wife of Mr. Samuel Dickinson,
who was drowned Sept. 3d, 1740
in the 36th year of her age,
And HEBZIBAH,
| Daughter of Mr. Samuel and
Mrs. Hannah Dickinson, |
who was drowned Sept. 3d, 1740
in the 8th year of her age.

Life glows and smiles with prospects bright,
Our life is doomed to care and toil,
Old age, the lonely eve of night,
Quick death writes vanity on all.

Quoted from "Bridgman's Epitaphs." The marble slab, supported by a sandstone table, is in fragments.

Dau. of John and Sarah (Coleman) Field, both of Hatfield.

Dickinson, 1778

Pamela Daughter of
Mr Thomas Wells &
Mrs Thankfull Dickinson who died July
21st 1778 in the 3^d
Year of her Age

Thomas Wells was s. of Thomas. Thankful was dau. Col. David Field.

Dickinson, 1780

[In memor]y of M^r
[SAMUE]L DICKIN-
[-SON] who died Nov^r [30th]
[1780 in] ye 45th year of
[his A]ge

the Soul depend
ent on the Dust
gives wings
above the spheres
gives the moral that was
the Prince of Peace.

This mutilated marble slab rests on a sandstone table monument.

S. of Samuel and Hannah (Field).

Dickinson, 1790

In Memory of Nancy
Daughter of David
and Elisabeth
Dickinson who die^d,
May 22^d, 1790. in
ye 5th Year of
her Age.

Dickinson, 1798

Daughter of
Mr Calvin &
Mrs Experienc^e
Dickinson died
Octr 8th 1798
aged 15 days.

Mrs. Experience was dau. of Simeon and Hannah (Hinsdale) Stebbins.

Dickinson, 1799

In Memory of
Betsey Daughter
to David and
Elizabeth Dick
inson, who died
June 5ᵗʰ 1799, in
the 16 Year of her
Age.

<small>Hark they whisper
Angels say, Sister
Spirits come away.</small>

Baptized Elizabeth, d. "of consumption."

Dickinson, 1808

To perpetuate the
Remembrance of Mrs
Elisabeth, Consort of
David Dickinson Esqʳ,
who died Janʸ 14ᵗʰ
1808, aged 62, Years.

<small>Mortals, how few among
our Race,
Have given this Thought
its Weight,
That on this fleeting Mome't
hangs,
Our everlasting State.</small>

Dau. of Rev. Jonathan and Dorothy (Williams) Ashley.

Dickinson, 1822

MAJOR
DAVID DICKINSON
A REVOLUTIONARY OFFICER
Died Dec. 15, 1822,
In his 75ᵗʰ Year

S. of Thomas and Prudence (Smith) of Bolton, Conn.

Felton, 1786

Memento Mori
Here Lies Buried
Mʳˢ Eunice Felton
Who quitted Mortality May 25ᵗʰ 1786
In the 38ᵗʰ year
of her Age.

Dau. of Elijah Williams and Lydia (Dwight) of Hatfield. Her husband was William, Jr. of Roxbury.

Field, 1747

In Memory of
Mʳˢ Mary Field,
the wife of Deaᶜⁿ
Samuel Field, she
Died July yᵉ 25ᵗʰ
1747. in yᵉ 70ᵗʰ Year
of her Age.

Samuel was s. of Samuel and Sarah (Gilbert). Mary was dau. of Joseph Edwards of Northampton. She m. (1) David Hoyt, who was k. in 1704. She was herself wounded at the Benoni Stebbins house.

DEERFIELD EPITAPHS

Field, 1762

In Memory of
Deac[n] SAMUEL
FIELD
who died au[t] 28th
1762. in y[e] 84th
Year of his age

<small>Hope humbly, then
with trembling Pinions
Soar; Wait ye Great tea;
cher Death & God
Adore</small>

S. of Samuel and Sarah (Gilbert) of Springfield.

Field, undated

Near the stones of Samuel (1747) and Mary (1762) are two small ones like foot stones marked
Mr.   Ebenezer
Sam[ll]   Field
Field

<small>They may be children of Samuel and Mary—"Mr. Samuel" perhaps b. 1708-9 who d. 1726 and Ebenezer b. 1723, whose life ended in twelve days.</small>

Field, 1792

DAVID FIELD Esqr.
died
April 19, 1792,
Aged 81 years

<small>These monuments* are gra-
-tuitously erected by their son in
law; Consider Dickinson.</small>

*This and that of his consort, Thankful.

S. of Samuel and Mary (Edwards | Hoyt).

Field, 1803

THANKFUL,
Consort of
David Field Esqr:
died
March 26, 1803,
aged 88 years.

Dau. of Thomas and Thankful (Hawks) Taylor. She may have been the consort first of Oliver Doolittle.

Forward, 1799

In Memory of Miss
Fanny A Forward
of Westfield, who
died May 16th 1799
in the 17th Year of
her Age.

<small>O'er the cold Turf where
thy pale Reliques sleep,
Shall fond Remembrance
oft repair to weep.</small>

Fanny Alumina, dau. of Rev. Abel and Dorothy —— of Southwick, originally part of Westfield. She d. in the family of Dea. Justin Hitchcock.

French, 1733

Here lyeth the body
of Deacon Thomas
French who dyed
April y[e] 5th 1733
Aged 76 Years

<small>Blessed are ye dead
Who dye in the Lord</small>

S. of John and —— Kingsley of Rehoboth.

French, 1759

In Memory of Mr
Thomas French
Who Died July 26
1759 In 69
Year of his Age

S. of Thomas and Mary (Catlin)

Graves, 1741, 1744

Mrs. Sarah Wife
of Mr John Graves
Died Jan^r 3. 1741.
Aged 79 Years.
Job Son of Mr. Da
niel & Mrs Thankful
Graves Died August
12 1744 aged 9 M.

Sarah, wife of John was dau. John White and Sarah (Bunce) all of Hatfield.
Job, her grandchild, s. of Daniel and Thankful (Smead).

Harvey, 1785

In Memory of
Mary the Wife of
Simeon Harvey
Who Departed this
Life December 20th
1785 In 39th year of
Her age on her left
Arm lieth the Infant
W^{h}ich was still
Born

Cut upon the stone is a coffin with figure of woman and infant.

Dau. Daniel and Mary (Stebbins) Arms.

Hawks, 1718, 1727

HERE LYES Y^e BODY OF
DEACON ELEAZER HAWKS
DYED MARCH Y^e 27th
1727 IN Y^e 72^d
YEAR OF HIS AGE
AND ALSO Mrs JUDETH
HAWKS WIFE TO DEACON
ELEAZER HAWKS DEC^d JAN^y
Y^e 27 1718 IN Y^e 54th
YEAR OF HER AGE.

S. of John and Elizabeth. Dau. of William Smead and Elizabeth (Lawrence) of Hingham.

Hawks, 1754

In Memory of
Mr. NATHANIEL
HAWKS who Di
ed Sep^t 25: 1754
In ye 56 Year
of his Age.

S. of Eliezer and Judith (Smead).

Hawks, 1768, 1774

A double Stone

Here Lies Inter^ed	Here lies inter'd
the Body of Dea^n	the Body of M^rs
ELEAZER	ABIGAIL the
HAWKS	Wife of Dea^n
Who Died	ELEAZER
May ye 14th	HAWKS
1774 Aged	who died
80 years	March ye 7th
	1768 Aged
	71 Years

By Virtue & Religion their lives they led
and in Peace they made the Grave their Bed

S. of Eleazer and Judith (Smead).   *Abigail (Wells).*

Hawks, 1769

In Memory of
Paul Son of M^r
Paul & Mrs Lois
Hawks, he Died
Jan^ry the 17th
1769. Aged
8 hours

Lois, mother of the baby, was a Wait of Hatfield.

Hawks, 1772

In Memory of Mrs Elizabeth,
Wife of Mr Seth Hawks,
she Died May ye 29th, 1772.
in the 41st Year
of her Age.

In Memory of Mr^s. Elisabeth,
Dau^tr of Mr Seth & Mrs Elisabeth Hawks she Died May y^e
16th 1772. in ye 19th Year of
her Age.

Seth was s. of Eleazer and Abigail (Wells). Mrs. Elizabeth dau. of Samuel and Elizabeth (Ingram of Hadley) Belding.

Hawks, 1775

In Memory of
Anne Daughter
of
Colonel John &
Mrs Elisabeth
Hawks who died
June 8th 1775
in ye 33^d
Year of her
Age.

Hawks, 1775

Elisabeth Dau^{tr}
of Mr. Zadok &
Mrs. Mary
Hawks Died
August 4th 1775
aged 5 Weeks

Zadock, s. of Nathaniel. Mary, dau. of Sam. Bardwell.

Hawks, 1778

In MEMORY of
Mr JOHN HAW-
KS who died Nov^r
21st 1778 in y^e
45th Year of
his Age

The Eye of her that
hath Seen me, Shall
see me no more.

S. of Col. John and Elizabeth (Nims).

Hawks, 1779

In Memory of
Mrs Elizabeth
Wife of Col.
John Hawks
who died Feb. 28
1779 aged 66.

Her Children arise
up & call her blessed
Pray, Kind reader lend an ear.
As you are now so once was I,
As I am now so must you be,
Prepare for Death and follow me.

Dau. of John and Elizabeth (Hull) Nims.

Hawks, 1780

In Memory of
Content Dau^r
of Mr Zadok
and Mrs Mary
Hawks who
died Jan 4th
1780 in the 12
Year of her
Age

Hawks, 1784

In Memory of
Col. John Hawks
who died June 24
1784. in the 77th
Year of his Age.

To be pious without super-
stition, faithful to our trust,
pleasant in our circle &
friendly to the poor, is to
imitate his example.

S. of Eleazer and Judith (Smead).

Hawks, 1785

In Memory of
Hannah Daugh-
-ter of Mr Zadoc
and Mrs Mary
Hawks who
died Octr 18th
1785 in the
24th Year
of her Age.

Hawks, 1787

Obed Son
of Mr Obed
& Mrs Abi
-gail Hawks
who died Feb
11th 1787 in the
2nd Month of
his Age.

*Obed, Sr. was s. of John and Eliz-
abeth (Nims). Mrs. Abigail
was born Smith of Belchertown.*

Hawks, 1791

Elissabeth Daut^r
of Mr Jonathan &
Mrs Mercy Haw^{ks}
who died Au
-gust 25th, 1791
in the 2^d Year of
her Age

Hawks, 1792

In Memory of M^r
Jonathan Hawks
who died Octr the
11th 1792 aged 29
Years 10 Months &
one Day

I am Laid into the Ground
and Left my Earthly pain,
Shall Rise when the Last
Trumpet Sounds and
meet with you again.

S. of Asa and Elizabeth (Smead).

Hawks, 1794

Abigail Dau^r
of Mr Obed &
Mrs Abigail
Hawks who died
July 26th 1794
in the 4th Year
of her Age.

Hawks, 1796

    In Memory
    of Wiman
    Son of M^r
    Zur & M^{rs}
    Martha Hawk^s
    who died July
    10th 1796 in the 2
    Year of his Age.

Grandson of Zadock. His mother was dau. of Daniel Arms.

Hawks, 1796

    In Memory of
    Chester Son of
    Mr Jonathan &
    Mrs Marcy Hawks
    who died
    1796 in
    Year of
(Lines imperfect because slate has scaled)

Marcy was a French of Greenfield.

Hawks, 1797

    In Memory
    of Esther
    Dau^r of M^r
    William & M^{rs}
    Abigail
    Hawks who
    died Angust
    29th 1797 in
    the 8th Month
    of her Age

William was s. of Seth. Abigail was born Marsh.

Hawks, 1817

    Mrs. Mary,
    Wife of
    Mr. Zadock Hawks,
    died
    4 Feb. 1817, Æ. 82

Dau. of Samuel and Martha (Allen) Bardwell.

Hawks, 1821

    Mr.
    Zadock Hawks
    died
    2 Aug. 1821 Æ.
    90

S. of Nathaniel and Hannah (Belding of Hatfield)

Hinsdell, 1735

    Here lyes buried
    the body of M^{rs}
    Abigail Hinsdell y^e
    amiable dau^r of
    The Revd M. Ebenezer
    Hinsdell & Mrs Abigail
    Hinsdell born Nov
    14. 1735. Dec^d
    Aug. 10th 1739, Æ 4to
    Mark 19 14. For of such is
    The Kingdom of Heaven

The Rev. and Col. Ebenezer, s. of Mehuman and Mary, was b. at sea when his mother was returning from Canada. Of H. C. 1727. He was sent to Ft. Dummer to serve the Indians, and founded the town of Hinsdale, opposite. "Mrs. Abigail" was dau. of Rev. John and Abigail (Allen | Bissell) Williams.

Hinsdell, 1736

HERE LYES BURIED THE BODY
OF LIEU^t MEHUMAN HINSDELL
DEC^d MAY Y^e 9th 1736.
IN THE 63^d YEAR OF HIS
AGE. WHO WAS THE FIRST
MALE CHILD BORN IN THIS
| PLACE AND WAS TWICE
CAPTIVATED |
BY THE INDIAN SALVAGES
Math. 5. 7 Blesed are the mercifull
for they shall obtain mercy

S. of Samuel and Mehitable (Johnson).

Hinsdell, 1736, 1746

In Memory of
Mr John Hinsdell,
Son of Mr Mehuman Hinsdell,
he Died Sep^t ye 4th 1746.
in the 33rd Year of his Age.
In Memory of Hannah Dau^{tr}
| of Mr John & Mrs Hannah
Hinsdell |
She Died Sep^t ye 6th 1736.
Aged 10 Days.

S. of Mehuman and Mary. Hannah, mother of the baby, was dau. of John Arms.

Hinsdell, 1788

IN
MEMORY
of
Mr John Hinsdell
who died Octr 20
1788, in the 51st
Year of his Age

S. of John and Hannah (Arms).

Hoit, 1751

In Memory of
Mrs Mercy y^e
Wife of Mr.
David Hoit
who Died Sep^t
5th 1751 in
the 28th year
of her Age.

Dau. of Ebenezer and Thankful (Barnard) Sheldon.

Hoit, 1758

Experience Daughter of Mr. Jonathan
& Mrs. Experience
Hoit Died Sep^t 19
1758. Aged 3 Year
& 10 Months.

Mr. Jonathan was son of David and Mercy (Sheldon). Mrs. Experience was dau. of Samuel and Experience Childs.

Hoit, 1758

    Cephas Son of
Mr. Jonathan &
Mrs. Experience
Hoit Died Oct 19
1758 Aged 1
year & 10 Month

Hoit, 1779

    In Memory of
Lieu^t Jonathan Hoit,
Who Dec^d ^{may} ye 23rd
1779 in ye 92nd Year
    of his Age

S. of David and Abigail (Cook | Pomeroy).

Hoit, 1780

    In Memory of
Mr^s Mary Hoit wife
to Lieu^t Jonathan Hoit
who Dec^d June ye 26th 1780
in ye 90th Year of her Age

Dau. of Samuel and Sarah (Gilbert) Field.

Hunter, 1787

    In Memory of Joh^n
Hunter Son of M^r
John & Mrs Elenor
Hunter who died
April 19th 1787 in
the 27th Year of
    his Age

Look and behold as you
Pass by as you are now so
once was I, as I am now so
you must be, Prepare for
Death and Follow me:

Locke, 1787

    In Memory:
of Mary Lock$_e$
Daughter of
Mr John and
Mrs Ruth Lock$_e$
who died June
25th 1787 iny^e
5th Year of her
    Age

John was s. of John of Woburn. Ruth dau. of Thomas and Joanna (Allen) Faxon.

Long, 1773

    In Memory of
Mr James Long,
he Died Augst y^e 9th 1773.
In y^e 24th Year
    of his Age.

Death is a debt to nature due,
Which i have Paid & so must you.

Merriman, 1757

Here Lies Interd
The Body of
M^s Mary Merriman
the wife of Ensign
Samuel Merriman
who Departed
this Life August
24 17 57
In ye 27 Year
of her Age

Mitchell, 1783

In Memory
of Mrs Mary
Wife of M^r
Joseph Mitch-
-ell who died
Novr 8th
1783 in the
78th Year of
her Age.

Dau. of William and Elizabeth (Davis) Allis of Sunderland.

Mitchell, 1794

In Memory of
Mr Joseph Mitch-
-ell who died
Septr 16th 1794.
in the 89th Year
of his Age.

S. of Michael and Sarah (Catlin).

Morgan, 1806

In Memory of
Mrs Marcy, Wife
of Mr. Jesse
Morgan, who
died June 8
1806, aged 37
Years.

Mun, 1767

In Memory of
Phinehas Son
of Mr Phinehas
& Mrs Dorothy
Mun he Died
Octr ye 28th 1767
Aged 5 Days

Phineas was s. of Benjamin and Mary (Wait). Dorothy was dau. of John and Mary (Munn) Catlin.

Munn, 1773

In Memory of
Merriam
Dau^{tr} of Mr Phinehas &
Mrs Dorothy Munn, she
Died Augst ye 10th 1773
Aged 1 Year & 15 Days.

Nims, 1754

In Memory of
Submit Dau^r
of Mr Jeremi-
ah & Mrs Mary
Nims Born &
Died July y^e
10th 1754

Jeremiah was s. of John and Elizabeth (Hull). Mary was dau. of Simon and Elizabeth (Gunn) Cooley of Sunderland. She d. 30 Apr. 1804.

Nims, 1754

The Body of
Mrs. Elisabeth y^e
Wife of Mr. John
Nims is here in-
terr'd: who Died
Sep^t 21. 1754 in y^e
66 Year of her age

Dau. of Jeremiah and Mehitable (Smead) Hull, who later m. Godfrey Nims, thereby making John and Elizabeth above, stepbrother and sister.

Nims, 1755

Mrs. Abigail
the Wife of Mr.
John Nims
Died Deec^m 4
A. D. 1755
Aged 38 Years

Dau. of Ebenezer and Esther (Catlin) Smead.

Nims, 1762

In Memory of
Mr John Nims
Who Died Dec.
29th A. D 1762
In the 83^d Year
of his Age

S. of Godfrey and Mary (Miller | Williams).

Nims, 1769

Mr. John
Nims Died
Oct. 6. A. D.
1769 In the
54th Year of
his Age.

S. of John and Elizabeth (Hull).

Nims, 1771

In Memory of M^{rs}
Mary the wife of
Mr Abner Nims,
who Died Octob^r
ye 26th 1771. in
ye 26th Year of her
Age

Dau. of Ebenezer and Mary (Hoyt) Sheldon.

Nims, 1778

Rebecah Dau^tr
of Mr. Israel
& Miss. Ruth
Nims died Dec.
13. 1778. aged
13 Months 3 ds

Israel was s. of Jeremiah and Mary (Cooley). Ruth, dau. of David and Rebecca (Arms) Childs.

Parker, 1786

In Memory of
Samuel Williams
Parker, Son of
Mr Isaac & M^rs
Deborah Parker,
who died July
7th 1786, Aged
1 Year & 3 Month

Isaac was of Boston. Deborah was dau. of Giles Alexander.

Phelps, 1793

Mrs. Rebekah Phelps,
died Nov. 1793; aged
72; 2^d Consort of Mr.
N. Phelps of Northampton.

When unaffected Christian Piety, and universal Benevolence, have crowned a long life, full of good works, let it be recorded on Marble, and faithfully transmitted to posterity.

As a tribute of gratitude to the memory of an indulgent Step-Mother, this Stone is erected by Elijah Phelps.

Russell, 1775

IN
MEMORY
of
Lieut. JOHN
RUSSELL
who died
August 17 1775
in the 44th
Year of his
Age.

S. of Elijah of Wetherfield.

Russell, 1808

Mr.
William Russell
died
6 Sep. 1808. Æ
46.

Son of Lieut. John and Hannah (Sheldon).

Russell, 1811

Mr.
ELIJAH RUSSELL
died
21 July 1811
Æ. 47

S. of John and Hannah (Sheldon).

Russell, 1814

Mrs.
HANNAH, Relict
of Lt. John Russell,
died 4 Feb. 1814
Æ. 76

*Dau. of John and Mercy (Arms)
Sheldon.*

Russell, 1862

ORRA HARVEY,
Wife of
ELIJAH RUSSELL,
DIED
Nov. 14, 1862,
Aged 89.

*Dau. of Simeon and Mary (Arms)
Harvey.*

Sexton, 1771

In Memory of
Mrs Sarah Sexton
Dau^{tr} of Mr Joseph &
Mrs Sarah Sexton
She Died April ye 7th
1771 in ye 35th Year
of her Age

*Mrs. Sarah (Parsons) was w. of
Joseph.*

Sexton, 1783

In Memory of
Mr John Sexton
who died Dec^{r}
26th 1783. in the
42nd Year of
his Age.

S. of Joseph and Sarah (Parsons).

Sexton, 1786

Rebecca Dau^{r} to M^{r}
David and M^{rs}
Bathsheba Sexton
died August 7
1786 in the 2nd
Year of her Age.
at the left hand lies
an Infant still born

Sexton, 1791, 1793

Theodorick Son to
Mr David & M^{rs}
Bathsheba Sexton
died July 20 1791 in
the 2nd Year of his
Age.
at the left hand lies
Theodorick the 2nd
died July 18 1793 in
the 2nd Year of his Age.

Sexton, 1800

Hon David Sexton
Esquire
died Septr 21st 1800
aged 66 years.
Why all this toil for tri-
umphs of an hour?
What tho' we wade in
wealth or soar in fame?
Earths highest station ends in
"Here he lies,"
And "dust to dust" concludes
her noblest song.

S. of Joseph and Sarah (Parsons).

Sexton, 1805

Mrs.
Rebecca Sexton,
Relict of
David Sexton Esq,
died July 18
1805,
Aged 77 Years.
Life makes the soul de-
-pendent on the dust;
Death gives her wings
to mount above the
spheres

Dau. Ebenezer and Anna (Foster) Barnard.

Saxton, 1824

DAVID SAXTON
died
Sept. 14, 1824,
Aged 61 years.
"May he rest in peace"

S. of David and Rebecca (Barnard)

Saxton, 1832

BATHSHEBA,
relict of
David Saxton,
died at Boston,
Oct. 20, 1832,
Æ. 68
"Blessed are the dead"

Dau. Thomas and Joanna (Allen) Faxon.

Shattuck, 1747

A small, mutilated stone
Jo   SH
E   14   1747

*Is doubtless that of Joseph Shat-
tuck, son of Samuel and Sarah
(Clesson) b. 6 Oct. 1745; d. 14
Feb. 1746/7.*

Sheldon, 1713

HERE LYES Y^e
BODY OF JOHN
SHELDON AGED
32 YEARS DEC^t
June ye 26th
1713

S. of John and Hannah (Stebbins).

Sheldin, 1724

EBEN[r]
SHELDIN
DYED ON Y[e]
27th OF IVNE 1724
AGED 22 YEAR

*S. of Ebenezer and Mary (Hunt).
Killed by Indians.*

Shelden, 1746

Here lies buried the
Body of M[rs] Thankf-
ul Shelden, the Wife of
Lieu[t] Ebenezer Sheld-
en, she Died Oct° y[e] 13th
Anno Dom: 1746. in the
52[d] Year of her Age

Death gives us more than was in Eden left
This king of terrors is the
prince of peace

*Dau. Joseph and Sarah (Strong)
Barnard.*

Sheldon, 1768

Mrs. MERCY
the Wife of Mr.
JOHN SHELDON
Died Feb[r] 7th
A. Dom. 1768
In y[e] 50 Year
of her Age

*Dau. of John and Hannah (Nash)
Arms.*

Shelden, 1793

In Memory of
M[r] John Shel-
-den who
died Dec[r] 4th
1793 in the 84th
Year of his Age.

Son of John and Hannah (Chapin).

Smead, 1733

HERE LYES Y[e] BODY OF
M[rs] EASTER SMEAD WIFE
TO M[r] EBENEZER SMEAD
DEC[d] DEC[r] Y[e] 12th 1733
IN Y[e] 59 YEAR
OF HER AGE

*Dau. of John and Mary (Baldwin)
Catlin.*

Smeed, 1753

In Memory of
Mr. EBENEZER
SMEED Who
Died July 19
1753. In the
79th Year of
His age.

*S. of William and Elizabeth (Law-
rence).*

Smith, 1778

Nancy Dau^tr of
Mr. Amasa & Miss.
Ruth Smith Died
August 6. 1778.
aged 11 Months &
12 Days.

Smith, 1781

Mrs. Ruth the
Wife of Mr.
Amasa Smith
Died Oct 20, 1781
in the 36 Year
of her age

Dau. John and Ruth (Catlin) Barnard.

Smith, 1793

In Memory of Abigal
Catlin Smith Dau^r
of Mr Moses & M^rs
Mary Smith, who
died April 27th 1793.
aged 8 Months &
22 Days.

Moses, s. of Moses and Sarah (Catlin. Mary, dau. of Samuel and Mary (Nims) Childs.

Smith, 1797

In Memory of
Ruth Barnard
Smith Dau^r of
Mr Amasa & M^rs
Naomy Smith
who died March
14th 1797 in the 13th
Year of her Age.

Sleep on my friend & take,
thy rest,
God call'd the home
he thought it best.

Named for Amasa's first wife. The child d. of hydrophobia. Mrs. Naomi m. (1) —— Dickinson.

Stebbins, 1733

Mrs. Mary the
Wife of Mr. John
Stebbins Died
in AD 1733
Aged 37 Years

Stebbins, 1760

In Memory of
Mr. JOHN STEB
BINS who Died
Sep^t ye 7th 1760
Aged 74 Years

S. of John and Dorothy (Alexander).

Stebbins, 1761

  lisabeth* ye Dau'tr
 of Mr. Joseph & Mrs
  Marah Stebbins
  Died August ye 8
  1761. Aged 2
  Years 5 Months
   & 20 Days.

*Note: The "E" is scaled off.

Stebbins, 1778

  Charlotte Dau^r
  of Capt Joseph
  & Mrs Lucy
  Stebbins who
  died August 27th
  1778: in the 2nd
  Year of her Age

Joseph was s. of Joseph. Lucy was dau. of Nathan and Eleanor (Warriner | Cooley | Barnard) Frary.

Stebbins, 1783

  In Memory of
  Samuel Son of
  Moses & Mercy
  Stebbins who
  Drowne^d decemb^r
  9th 1783 In the 18
  Year of his age

Stebbins, 1785

  In Memory of
  Mrs Mercy Wife
  To Mr Moses
  St^{e}bbins who die^d
  May 1st 1785 In
  the 51st Year of
   Her age

Dau. of Eleazer and Abigail (Wells) Hawks, bap. and bur. as Mercy. She seems to have been called Dorcas.

Stebbins, 1797

  This Monument is
  Erected to the
  Memory of M^r
  Joseph Stebbins
  who Departed
  this Life May the
  30th 1797, in the
  79th Year of his
   Age.

Were I so tall to reach the
Pole, Or grasp the Oce
an with a Span,
I must be measur'd by
my Soul,
The Mind's the Standard,
of the Man.

S. of John and Hannah (Allen).

Stebbins, 1797

This Monument is
Erected to the
Memory of M^rs
Mary Stebbins
Consort of M^r
Joseph Stebbins
who Depar'ed
this Life July the
2nd 1797. in the
72nd Year of her
Age

*Dau. of Hezekiah and Elizabeth
(Hawks) Stratton of Northfield.*

Stebbins, 1800

Here lies the
Remains of M^r
Moses Steb-
-bins Junr
who died Dec^r
14th 1800, in the
39th Year of
his Age.

And when the last
Trumpet sounds,
Arise come forth ye
Dead, The call shall
be to them & all, That
sleep in dusty beds.

*S. of Moses and Mercy (Hawks).
"Frozen to death," says Mr.
Sheldon's history.*

Stebbins, 1804

In Memory of
Mrs Experience
Wife of Mr
Moses Stebbins,
who died Sept
30 1804,
aged 64 Years.

Dau. of —— Clark of Northampton.

Stebbins, 1815

In memory of
Moses Stebbins,
who died
15, Nov. 1815;
Æ. 85.

S. of John and Hannah (Allen).

Tyler, 1756

In Memory of
Christopher Son of
Mr Christopher & M^rs
Lucy Tyler he Died
Sep^t ye 4th 1756. Aged
1 Year 6 Months

*Mrs. Lucy was dau. of Benjamin
and Mary (Wait) Munn.*

Wells, 1697

HERE LYES BURIED
THE BODY OF M^{rs}
HEPZIBAH WELLS WIFE
TO JONATHAN WELLS ESQ^r
DIED AUG^t Y^e 27th
1697. IN THE 37th
YEAR OF HER AGE

Dau. Quartermaster George Colton of Springfield and Deborah (Gardner) of Hartford.

Wells, 1733/4

HERE LYES Y^e BODY OF
Mrs SARAH WELLS WIFE
TO Mr JONATHAN WELLS
DEC^d FEB^{ry} ye 10th 1733/4
IN ye 77th YEAR
OF HER AGE

Dau. of John and Abigail (Ford) Strong of Northampton, wid. of Joseph Barnard.

Wells, 1735

HERE LYES BURIED
Y^e BODY OF Mr JONATIAN
WELLS WHO DIED
MAY Y^e 27th 1735.
IN THE 52^d YEAR
OF HIS AGE.

S. of Jonathan and Sarah (Strong | Barnard).

Wells, 1738

HERE LYES BURIED
THE BODY OF
JONATHAN WELLS
ESQ^r WHO DEC^d
JAN^{ry} THE 3^d 1738
IN THE 80th YEAR
OF HIS AGE.

S. of Thomas and Mary (Beardsley).

Wells, 1743

Here lyes Buried the Body
of Doct^r THOMAS WELLS
who Departed this Life
March the 7th Anno Dom
1743 in ye 51st Year
of His Age.

S. of Ebenezer and Mary (Wait).

Wells, 1746

In Memory of Benjamin,
Son of Doc^{tr} Thomas &
Mr^s Sarah Wells, he
Died March ye 28th 1746
in the 16th Year
of his Age.

Behold my grave as you Pass by,
for as you are so once was I.
Death Suddenly took hold on me,
and so the case with you may be.

Wells, 1750

In Memory of
Mr Jonathan
Wells Who Dec^d
Octr ye 30th 1750
in ye 27th Year
of his Age

S. of Jonathan and Mary (Hoyt).

Wells, 1750

In Memory of
Mrs Mary, Relict
of E^{n}sign Jonatha^n
Wells who Dec^d
nov^{br} ye 22nd 1750
in ye 48th year of her
Age.

Dau. of David and Mary (Edwards of Northampton) Hoyt.

Wells, 1751

In Memory of
Mrs Rebecca Wells
Daug^{tr} of Ensign
Jonathan & M^{rs}
Mary Wells She
Dec^d Jan^{ry} ye 9th
1751 in ye 17th Year
of her Age.

Ens. Jona. was s. of Jonathan. Mrs. Mary was born Hoyt.

Wells, 1754

In Memory of
Mr Oliver Wells
who Dec^d Oct^r
ye 1^t 1754 in y^e
22^d Year of his Age

S. of Jonathan and Mary (Hoyt).

Wells, 1758

Here is Interr'd
ye Body of Ens'^{n}
Ebenezer Wells
Who Died June
ye 12. 1758. In
the 67th Year
of his Age.

S. of Ebenezer and Mary (Wait).

Wells, 1758

In Memory of
Samuel Son of
Samuel Wells
Esqr & M^{rs}
Hannah his Wife
he Dec^d oct^r y^e,
3rd 1758, Aged
18 Months & 2
D

Samuel Sr. was s. of Jonathan. Mrs. Hannah was dau. Ebenezer and Thankful (Barnard) Sheldon.

Wells, 1779

This to perpetuate
the Memory of Mr.
Zeeb Wells Son of
Mr. Ebenezer & Mrs.
Mercy Wells who
Died Oct° 6th 1779
Aged 17 Years and
3 Months.

By Youthful Ashes See
What Soon your State will be.

Died "through bleeding at the nose." Ebenezer s. of Thomas. Mercy dau. Samuel Bardwell.

Wells, 1783

In Memory of
Mr Ebenezer Wells
who died July 23rd
1783 in the 53rd
Year of his
Age

S. of Thomas and Sarah (Hawks).

Wells, 1783

In Memory
of
Mrs SARAH WELLS Relict
of
THOMAS WELLS Physician
who died Octr ye 10th 1783
In ye 83d Year of Her Age

Blessed are the dead which
die in the Lord. Rev. 14th 13th

Dau. Eleazer and Judith (Smead) Hawks.

Wells, 1786

In Memory of
Mr Augustus Wells
Son of Doctr Thomas
& Mrs Sarah Wells
who deceased July ye
16th 1786 in the 53rd
Year of his
(Earth line)

Wells, 1791

In Memory of
Mrs Anna Wells
Wife of
Mr Ebenezer Wells,
who died Septr 20th
1791, aged 31
Years.

Dau. of David and Rebecca (Barnard) Saxton.

Wells, 1793

In Memory of
Mr Ebenezer Wells,
who died December
23rd 1793. in the
36th Year of his
Age.

S. of Ebenezer and Mercy (Bardwell).

Wells, 1801

In Memory of
Mrs Marcy Wells,
Consort of
Mr Ebenez'r Wells,
who died March
29th 1801, in the
64th Year of her
Age.

*Dau. of Samuel and Martha
(Allen) Bardwell.*

Williams, 1703-4

Here lyeth the Body of
Mrs Eunice |
Williams the Vertuo^{n}s
& desirable |
Consort of the Revrd Mr John
Williams, & Daughter to ye Revrd
Mr Eleazer & Mrs Esther Mather
of Northampton. She was Born
Augt 2. 1664. and fell by the
rage of ye Barbarous Enemy
March 1. 1703/4.

Prov: 31. 28. Her Children arise
up & Call her Bless'd;

Williams, 1714

HERE LYES Y^e
BODY OF JOHN
WILLIAMS SON
TO Y^e R^d JOHN
AND ABIGAIL
WILLIAMS AGED
5 YEARS DEC^d
JUNE 11th 1714

Williams, 1729

Here lyes ye Body of the
Revd Mr John Williams
the Beloved & Faithfull
Pastor of this place. Who
dyed on June ye 12 1729
In the 65th Year of his age

Rev 14 13 Write Blessed
are ye Dead which die
in the Lord.

S. of Samuel and Theoda (Parke).

Williams, 1738

SARAH WILLIAMS
Y^e DAUGH^r OF M^r
ELIJAH AND M^{rs}
LYDIA WILLIAMS;
DIED APRIL 4th
1738: AGED 2
MONTHS & 1 DAY

Williams, 1746

Here lies interred
ye Body of
Mrs. ANNE,
ye Wife of
Dr. THOMAS WILLIAMS,
who died May 6, 1746,
In ye 23 year of her age.

This stone was erected in 1862,
in place of one erected in 1746

Dau. Timothy and Hannah (Chapin | Sheldon) Childs.

Williams, 1750

Here lies Interd ye Body of
Mrs Sybil Williams,
the Daughter of
Elijah Williams Esqr
and Mrs Lydia His Wife;
who Died Octr ye 15th
1750 in ye 15th
Year of Her Age.

Williams, 1754

Here lies intere'd the Body of
Mrs Abigail Williams,
the Relict of the
Revd Mr JOHN WILLIAMS of
this Place: She Died June y^e
| 21st 1754: in the 82^d
Year of Her Age |

Dau. of Thomas and Abigail (Warham) Allen, and wid. of Benj. Bissell.

Williams, 1754

In Memory of
Col^o Ephraim Williams
Esqr of Stockbridge.
who Died Augst ye 11th
1754. in ye 63^d
Year of his Age

Blesst be that Hand divine, which gently laid my Heart at rest beneath this humble Shed.

S. of Isaac and Judith (Hunt | Cooper) of Rehoboth. His son Ephraim,1715-1755, was founder of Williams College.

Williams, 1756

HERE LIES Y^e BODY OF
Mrs SARAH WILLIAMS,
THE DAU^r OF
ELIJAH WILLIAMS ESQ^r
& Mrs LYDIA HIS WIFE:
SHE DIED JUNE Y^e 14th
1756: AGED 13 YEARS.

Williams, 1757

Ephraim Son of
Thomas Willi
ams Esq. & Mrs.
Esther Williams
Died Augst 1st
1757. Aged 12
Days.

Williams, 1759

Esther Daughter
of Thomas Willi
ams Esq. & Mrs
Esther Williams
Died July 27th
1759. Aged 6
Months 9 Days

Williams, 1771

In Memory of Major Elijah Williams Esqr who Died July the 10th 1771. in the 59th Year of his Age.

S. of Rev. John and Abigail (Allen | Bissell). He m. (1) Lydia Dwight of Hatfield, (2) Margaret Pynchon.

Williams, 1771

In Memory of Horace Son of Thomas Williams Esqr & Mrs Esther Williams, who Died Novr ye 13th 1771. Aged 2 Months & 11 Days

Williams, 1772

Here lies the Body of Mrs MARGARET WILLIAMS, the virtuous Relict of ELIJAH WILLIAMS Esqr She died April 15th AD 1772 in the 45th Year of her Age.

Dau. of William and Katharine (Bremer) Pynchon of Springfield.

Williams, 1775

In Memory of Thomas Williams Esq; Who died Sept: 28, 1775. Æt. 57.

To each unthinking being, Heaven, a
(friend,
Gives not the useless Knowledge of its
(end;
To man imparts it; but with such a
(view,
As, while he dreads it, makes him
(hope it too.

S. of Ephraim and Elizabeth (Jackson). Sometimes called Dr. Thomas.

Williams, 1777

In Memory of John Son of Mr John & Mrs Eliza^{beth} Williams he Dec^d Augst ye 20th 1777 Aged 1 year.

Williams, 1781

In Memory of Jonathan Son to Wm Williams Esqr and Mrs Dorothy Williams who die^d Feby 27th 1781 Aged 6 Months

This is the third little stone on which is cut a coffin. See Ashley, 1779.

Williams, 1785

In Memory of
Mrs Elizabeth Williams
Wife of
Mr John Williams,
who died July 27th 1785.
Aged 30 Years.

John was s. of Elijah and Margaret (Pynchon). Mrs. Elizabeth was dau. of Jonathan Orne of Salem.

Williams, 1793

In Memory of
Elijah Williams Esqr
who died March 24th AD 1793,
Aged 48 Years.

S. of Elijah and Lydia (Dwight).

Williams, 1796

Richard William^s,
Son of
John & Elizabeth
Williams
died Octr 15
1796,
Aged 21 Years.

Williams, 1800

Mrs Esther Williams,
relict of
Thomas Williams
Esquire,
died Septr 24th 1800
aged 74 years.

Life is the Triumph of our
mould'ring Clay,
Death, of the Spirit
infinite! divine!

Dau. of Rev. William and Hannah (Stoddard) Williams of Weston. These two, son and dau. of the ministers of Hatfield and Northampton, were mar. by "one of Her Majesties Council." Esther was married by her father, civil marriages being less usual.

Williams, 1911

William Stoddard Williams
June 25 1834
August 19 1911

Our fathers trusted in thee: they
trusted and thou didst deliver them.

S. of Ephraim and Rebecca (Jackson).

Wright, 1747

In Memory of M^r
Judah Wright
who died August
30th 1747 in the
72^d Year of his
Age. He was one
of the unfortunate
persons who was captured by the Indians
Feb 29th 1703-4.

S. of Judah and Mercy (Burt).

Wright, 1758, 1762, 1763, 1770

In Memory of the
Children of Deacon Asa
el & M⁽ʳˢ⁾ Lucy Wright.

| Lois Died Nov⁽ʳ⁾ y⁽ᵉ⁾ 8ᵗʰ 1758 Aged 2 Years & 7 Days | Ruben Died Feb⁽ʳʸ⁾ y⁽ᵉ⁾ 26ᵗʰ 1762 Aged 1 Year & 1 Month | A Son Still Born April y⁽ᵉ⁾ 5ᵗʰ 1763 | Judah Died Jan⁽ʳʸ⁾ y⁽ᵉ⁾ 18ᵗʰ 1770 Aged 10 Years & 10 Months |

Asahel, s. of Judah and Mary (Hoyt). Lucy, dau. of Joseph Wait of Hatfield and widow of Reuben Bardwell.

Wright, 1769

In Memory of
M⁽ʳˢ⁾ Mary Wright,
the Wife of M⁽ʳ⁾
Judah Wright, she
Died July y⁽ᵉ⁾ 23⁽ᵈ⁾
1769 Aged 89
Years.

Dau. of David and Sarah (Wilson) Hoyt.

Wright, 1797

In Memory of
Lucy Dau⁽ʳ⁾ of
M⁽ʳ⁾ Asahel & M⁽ʳˢ⁾
Miranda Wright
who died July
19ᵗʰ 1797 in
the 4ᵗʰ Year of
her Age.

Wright, 1797

In Memory of
Deacon Noah
Wright who
died Nov 7 1797
in the 81ˢᵗ year
of his Age.
Let the Witling Argue all
He can,
It is Religeon still that
makes the Man.

S. of Judah and Mary (Hoyt).

Wright, 1798

This Monument is
Erected to the
Memory of M⁽ʳˢ⁾
Miranda Consort
of M⁽ʳ⁾ Asahel
Wright Jun⁽ʳ⁾ who
died March 6 1798
in the 31ˢᵗ Year of
her Age.

Asahel was s. of Asahel and Lucy (Wait | Bardwell). Mrs. Miranda was b. Wetherby.

Wright, 1806
    In Memory of
W^d Esther, Relict
of Deacon Noah
Wright, who died
Octr 24 1806,
aged 91 Years
*Dau. of William and Elizabeth
Scott of Hatfield.*

Two unidentified stones are marked:

    M. T. 17 and

    S S D F 1700

In a common grave in the south-eastern corner of the ground were buried the victims of the massacre. On one side of the stone which crowns the mound is:

THE DEAD OF

1704

On the reverse:

THE GRAVE OF
48 MEN WOMEN AND
CHILDREN, VICTIMS
OF THE FRENCH AND
INDIAN RAID ON
DEERFIELD,
FEBRUARY 29, 1704

The list of names which follows, of those "who were slain at the Taking of the Town," was "drawn up by the Rev. Stephen Williams of Springfield [Longmeadow] soon after his Return from Captivity" and was printed in "The Redeemed Captive."

ALEXANDER, DAVID, s. of John and Beatrice.
ALLIS (ELLICE), SAMUEL, soldier of Hatfield, s. of Samuel and Alice.
BOLTWOOD, SERGT. SAMUEL. Soldier of Hadley.
" ROBERT. Soldier of Hadley.
CARTER, THOMAS, (4), s. of Samuel and Mercy (Brooks).
CATLIN, JOHN, s. of John and Isabella (Ward).
" JOSEPH, k. in Meadow Fight, and
" JONATHAN, sons of John (above) and Mary (Baldwin).
FIELD, SARAH, (10 mos.), dau. John and Mary (Bennett).
FOOT, SAMUEL. Soldier of Hatfield.
FRARY, SAMSON, s. of John and Prudence.
FRENCH, JOHN, (4 weeks), child of Thomas and Mary (Catlin).
HAWKS, ALICE, w. of John, Sr.
" JOHN, JR. (30), s. John and Martha (Baldwin).
" THANKFUL (SMEAD), his w. and all their children, viz:
" JOHN, (7).
" MARTHA, (4).
" THANKFUL, (2).
HINSDALE, SAMUEL, (15 mos.), s. of Mehuman and Mary.
HOYT, DAVID, (29), s. of David and Abigail (Cook | Pomeroy).
INGRAM, JONATHAN, (27). Soldier of Hadley.
INGERSOL, JOSEPH, (28).
KELLOGG, JONATHAN, (5), s. of Martin and Sarah (Dickinson | Lane).
MATTOON, REBECCA (NIMS), (24), w. of Philip, who was k. on the journey.
" Their infant son. Mother and child were burned in a cellar, says S. Williams' MS.
PARTHENA, servant of Mr. Williams.
NIMS, HENRY, (22).
" MEHITABLE, (7).
" MARY, (5).
" MERCY, (5), all children of Godfrey and Mary (Miller | Williams). The little girls were burned in the house.
PRICE, SARAH, w. of Robert, dau. of John Webb and previously married to Zech. Field.

ROOT, MERCY, (15), dau. Hezekiah and Mehitable (Frary).
An orphan, living with her grandfather, Samson Frary.
SELDEN, THOMAS, (26), s. of Thomas and Felix (Lewis).
SHELDON, HANNAH (STEBBINS), (39), w. of John.
" MERCY, (2), her child.
SMEAD, ELIZABETH (LAWRENCE), (64?), w. of
William. Her daughter-in-law.
" MARY (PRICE), (23), w. of Samuel
and Mary's two children:
" SARAH, (4).
" WILLIAM, (2). All were smothered in the cellar of the burning house.
SMITH, MARTIN, (50?), perished in cellar of John Hawks's house.
STEBBINS, BENONI, (51), s. of John and Mary (Munden): prob. Munson.
STEVENS, ANDREW, an Indian.
WAIT, SERGT. BENJAMIN, of Hatfield.
WARNER, NATHANIEL, of Hadley.
WELLS, MARY, (30), dau. of Thomas and Hepzibah (Buel). In 1693 she was "knocked on the head and scalped," but recovered to be scalped again.
WILLIAMS, JOHN, (6).
" JERUSHA, (6 weeks). Children of Rev. John and Eunice (Mather).

www.ingramcontent.com/pod-product-compliance
Lightning Source LLC
Chambersburg PA
CBHW070426080426
42450CB00030B/1622